ONE MORE
SHOT
Take It and Make It Count

by Steve Miller

One More Shot

Cover Art & Interior: Navigation Advertising

First Edition

CONTENTS

INTRODUCTION

Life is full of opportunities. In the course of our lives, we experience opportunities pertaining to education, employment, relationships, and so much more. But an opportunity in and of itself does not guarantee anything other than potential. Often, success or failure depends entirely on how we approach each opportunity. The goal of this book is to help you take full advantage of the next opportunity — the next *shot!* — that comes your way.

When I decided to write this book, I thought its purpose would be primarily for individuals. The goal of improving oneself and taking advantage of the opportunities one experiences is often a very individualistic experience in terms of the immediate effects of such an undertaking. To that end, there is no question that when you implement the practices I share in this book, your odds of making the next shot count will greatly increase.

However, as the book took shape, I realized the greater implications of what is contained herein are very much communal in nature. I believe this book will not only impact the individual reader, but by default, if the reader implements the practices I recommend, they will produce a ripple effect that will inspire others, strengthen relationships, foster positive change, promote teamwork, and facilitate network change.

The implications of those five ripple effects are
as follows:

Inspiring Others: As others witness you implement and
develop the structures found herein, you will inspire them
to step out of their comfort zones and set out on their
own road to improvement.

Strengthening Relationships: As you grow, you will
begin to foster empathy, and your communication
with others — as well as your own attitude — will
improve. This will lead to deeper connections with others
based on mutual trust, respect, and understanding.
Stronger, healthier relationships will provide life-giving
encouragement and lead to greater accountability.

Fostering Positive Change: Positive change within the
life of an individual extends powerfully to the community.
As you improve, you will focus less on yourself and more
on those around you. This awareness will lead to action,
and the actions you take will have a lasting impact
on society.

Promoting Teamwork: As growth occurs, you will begin
to surround yourself with others who buy into your cause
and support you as you make your next shot count.
It is through teamwork and team growth that the
"dream works."

Facilitating Network Change: This one will seem selfish, but it's not. Your desire to become a person who has developed the disciplines necessary to take and make your shot count will allow you to move into new social networks. These new networks in which you operate will serve as a catalyst by which your ripples can turn into waves. Ed Mylett famously said, "You are one person away from changing your family's future in the best possible way for generations to come." New networks established through the shared goal of making every shot count leads to a heightened sense of accountability.

The practices contained in this book are the result of years of trial and error, studying under those who have experienced success in life, and the desire to learn from my own experiences. These are not just theories to me, they are principles obtained as a result of a lifetime spent in pursuit of making the next shot count. The impact of applying the principles is real and long-lasting. Your life and the lives of those around you will be impacted when you make the decision to apply the structures you find here. I look forward to hearing the story of how you made your next shot count. I hope you enjoy the book.

Everyone deserves *One More Shot.*

DEDICATION

This book is dedicated to Cindy Miller, my wife and courage provider for 31 years. She is the reason I have the mental energy to take the next shot. She prefers to stay behind the scenes most of the time. She is the definition of faithfulness. She is loving, strong, humble, smart, and kind. Best of all, she loves me.

ONE MORE SHOT
Take It and Make It Count

The gym was packed, and the game was close.
The winners would move on to host the area tournament
with home-court advantage in the sub-regionals. With less
than 15 seconds left, we took the lead by three points.
I yelled to a member of our team, "Foul him!" He fouled
an opponent, and the official called an intentional foul.
This meant that the other team would take two free
throws and get the ball back.

Their player made both free throws, they inbound the
ball, ran a play effectively, and scored.

In a matter of seconds, we moved from what appeared
to be a sure win to a certain loss. With less than three
seconds remaining, we'd have to go the full length of the
court and score in order to win. Devastated, I called for a
time-out, and as the players approached the bench,
I started apologizing.

"Hey, my bad, we should have just played defense.
You deserve to win this game. I'm sorry guys, I cost us
this one."

Then, I heard a voice say, "Coach, we have time for one
more shot. What do you have for us? We can still

NOTES

win this." Like a bolt of lightning, his words caught my attention.

We have time for one more shot.

With renewed focus, I called a play we practiced often for this very situation, a play designed to get the ball to our best shooter. When it came time to run the play, our opponents defended him well, so we passed the ball to the only available player. He had only one option, and it was a longshot, but with seconds left on the clock, he took it. As his feet left the ground and he sent the ball flying through the air, time stood still. Everything went into slow motion.

Swish. Nothing but net. A perfect three-point shot.

"One more shot" won the game.

As we celebrated our victory, the words of my player echoed in my head: "Coach, we have time for one more shot. We can still win this." As I drove home, I thought long and hard about the lesson I learned in that high school gym that night. To this day, I find the concept to be profound: So long as there's time on the clock, we have a chance.

I love concepts. They're beautiful things. There's life-changing potential in a concept. However, if a concept is never challenged — never put to the test — it's nothing more than an abstract idea. It's one thing to have a

NOTES

concept in your mind, but it's another thing entirely to encounter a life event that forces you to walk out that principle in real time. A concept without action serves little purpose.

For me, this catalyst came in the form of a dead end on the career path I had pursued my entire professional life. I was at the top of my game and functioning at the highest level in my job. I was thinking about taking the next step which would move me to the very top of my profession. Then, through a series of choices, I left work on Friday and never returned. A 27-year career came to a hard stop. Like a car hitting a wall, that part of my life ended. It was a struggle to say the least. After all the hard work and the time I spent building this part of my life, the sudden stop took my breath away.

As the shock began to fade over the course of the next few days, questions began to surface, and I came face-to-face with the "if only" and the "what-ifs." My mind turned against me, and I did a lot of mental tossing and turning, desperately seeking answers. I'm embarrassed to say it took longer than it should have, but in the end, that crisis challenged me to take action. It reminded me that there was still time on the clock.

"I'm still here," I told myself. "I still have time." If I still had time, I still had a chance. "I may be down by two with only three seconds left in the game, but there's time for another play."

NOTES

I began to rebuild my confidence with that thought. My mindset shifted from the things I didn't like about my circumstances to the blessings I could count on. I realized the value of family and friends. I began to devote more attention to being the type of husband my wife deserves. I became, and am in the process of becoming, a much more productive follower of Jesus. In doing so, my gratitude increased, and I became more disciplined. I began to bury bad habits and replace them with better ones. I learned how to change a bad attitude, and I looked for — and found! — a great coach of my own.

This decision to take that concept, inspired that day on the basketball court, and put some action to it, helped me develop a One More Shot mentality. As a result of this total shift in my mindset, I have a happy marriage, a growing business, and I'm surrounded by family and friends I love who love me back. I'm also living my dream of coaching businesses and individuals who are currently reaping the benefits of a life lived with a One More Shot mindset.

The strategies outlined in this book have helped me find value and purpose in everything I set my mind to do. The rewards reaped from this lifestyle allow me to do the things I enjoy — to hunt where I want to hunt, to live in the house I want to live in, and to enjoy the truck I drive. God is Great. Life is Good!

NOTES

Acknowledging that a concept is no good unless it is accompanied by action, I encourage you to read this book and put into practice the One More Shot philosophy in your own life. I can tell you from experience that even if your life is going great, it can change in an instant. What you are currently experiencing can — and for many, will — change and put you in an unexpected One More Shot situation. When this happens, you will be well-served to have these proven strategies in place in your life.

For those who feel you are down to your last shot and need to make this one count, this book is for you. It will not be easy, and it will take commitment on your part, but if you choose to take action, you will change for the better, and you will improve your odds of making the shot you take.

NOTES

CHAPTER 1
It All Starts With Time
How ONE MORE SHOT People Treat Time

In a world where people waste time in more ways than can be counted, One More Shot people spend, view, and use time differently.

Here are the five ways One More Shot people handle time differently:

1. **They view time as a gift.**
2. **They use time to gain an advantage.**
3. **They are intentional with their time.**
4. **They understand *now* is the right time.**
5. **They realize time is always running out.**

One More Shot People View Time as a Gift

Time is a gift from God. We need to make sure we treat it like the precious gift it is. In the Bible, James makes a profound comment about time. He writes, "Yet you do not know what tomorrow will bring. What is your life? For you are a mist that appears for a little while and then is a vapor" (James 4:14, ESV).

NOTES

The gift of time is an opportunity. Revered University of Alabama Coach Paul Bear Bryant understood the value of time. He always carried this poem with him:

The Beginning of a New Day

This is the beginning of a new day. God has
given me this day to use as I will.

I can waste it or use it for good.

What I do today is important because I am
trading a day of my life for it.

When tomorrow comes, this day will be
gone forever leaving something in its place
I have traded for it.

I want it to be gain not loss — good not evil.
Success not failure,

In order that I shall not regret the price
I have paid for it.

An individual who operates under the One More Shot mentality must take the gift of time seriously.

Our grandson was about 18 months old the Christmas of 2023, and as you can imagine, he received way more gifts

NOTES

than he needed at that age. I watched him open each gift, so excited as he opened one gift after another. Today, I imagine he no longer remembers the gifts he received in 2023. At his age, he simply doesn't grasp the value of a gift beyond the initial excitement of opening it. More often than not, this perspective changes with age.

Take my wife, for example. During the Christmas of 2023, she was in a much different place than any she had experienced in her life. Her mother had passed the year before, and my wife was still grieving as she managed the process of selling the family home. For Christmas, our daughter gave her a very nice custom picture of the homeplace that factored in so many of my wife's sweetest memories. My wife cried when she opened it. She cherishes those memories dearly, and the excitement of this gift lingered long after she unwrapped it.

She immediately searched the house until she found just the right spot to hang it, a spot where she would see it every day. To this day, that gift has not lost its value. She recalls not only the opening of the gift itself but the memories she cherishes from the house in the picture.

Time, taking the form of a gift, can be received in mature and immature ways. We all receive the gift. What matters is what we do with it. Will we open it and move on, allowing our circumstances or emotions to dictate how seriously we take the gift? Or will we conscientiously consider its value every day?

NOTES

Time is a gift to us from God. However, we cannot control it and we have no idea how much of it we will be given. A One More Shot individual understands this and is continuously thankful for the gift.

Key questions:

Are you treating the gift of time like a toddler, or are you viewing it like my wife views the precious picture of her homeplace?

Are you trading your time for something good that will bring joy to your life and to others?

NOTES

One More Shot People Are Mindful of Gaining Time Advantages

Regardless of age, race, gender, wealth, talent, etc., we all have one thing in common. We are all given the same amount of time in a day, an hour, a minute. While we all have the same amount of time, we do not all use time in the same way. The time we are given, when used wisely, can help us gain advantages. The late Kobe Bryant harnessed this power. His perspective on time and his drive are evident in how he lived his life. In a well-known interview, he said:

"You wake up at 3 a.m., train 4 to 6, come home, eat breakfast, relax. Now you are back at it again, 2 to 4 p.m. Back at it again 7 to 9 p.m. By the years 5 and 6, it does not matter what kind of work they do in the summer — they are never going to catch up."

As you become a One More Shot person, look for ways you can use time to gain an advantage. It may be as simple as getting up a little earlier. Or it could be forming a daily habit that allows you to consistently do things that separate you from your competition. Most likely, it will involve making sure you can add time every chance you get. What does that look like?

Coach Michael Burt owns a private jet that allows him to do multiple events in one day. It also allows him to get home quickly when he is finished for the day or the

NOTES

week. So, while his competition waits at the airport, he is at the next meeting or headed home to his wife and kids. Three or four years of this will separate him from his competitors. He is using the jet to gain a time advantage.

While most of us will never enjoy the luxury of a private jet, we all can maximize the tools available to us to make the best use of the time we've been given. How can you better use your cellphone to conduct business when you're commuting to free up your time at home to focus on the family? Perhaps you can listen to audio books while doing those mundane but necessary chores that require little focus. Invest in technology that frees up your time and spend less time scrolling through social media.
Get creative. Don't assume creating more time will require a substantial financial investment.

Key questions:

In what areas are you currently using time to gain an advantage?

What are some key areas of your life where you can use time to gain an advantage?

NOTES

One More Shot People Use Time Intentionally

The world will tell you that to be successful, you need to manage your time. One More Shot people understand that time cannot be managed. Time is linear. It keeps moving forward. No one can control it or change it. It can, however, be used intentionally. This concept is extremely important if you desire to have a life full of great experiences and make great memories. In order to take that dream trip, start that new business, or break that bad habit, you need more than good intentions.

So many people genuinely *want* to do great things, but they spend their lives intending to do them rather than actually doing them. More often than not, time is usurped by obligations and circumstances. Great ideas and big dreams are delayed when the time needed to accomplish them is spent doing something else. Time is much like money; when not appropriately budgeted, it seems to disappear. Extraordinary intentions are a dime a dozen, and if they simply remain good intentions, one day you will be out of time.

We need a better way — a new outlook on the subject of time. To that end, I propose that time be treated like a wise investor treats money. Great investors are very intentional with the process and placement of money. They have a very clear approach to how they handle each dollar. Time should be handled in the same fashion. The time required to accomplish the most important tasks

NOTES

should be blocked out and cemented in your
daily schedule.

Steven R. Covey once said, "If the big rocks do not go
in first, they aren't going to fit in later." In other words,
if you do not intentionally block off time for important
things, those things will never be accomplished.

One More Shot people replace their to-do lists with a
carefully planned calendar that has specific time slots
reserved daily for the most important things in their lives.
Adherence to the calendar ensures their time is used in a
manner that enables them to accomplish their dreams —
to take that trip, to start that new business, to beat that
bad habit, to visit those faraway friends and family. The
calendar takes an intention from an idea to reality.

Key Questions:

What are you doing with the time you have been given?

Have you put your good intentions to action, using your
time effectively each day, or is it simply passing without a
plan?

Do your daily and yearly calendars reflect an intentional
use of time?

NOTES

One More Shot People Understand the Right Time to Do Anything Important is Now

How many times in life have you looked at an opportunity and thought *if I had this or that ready, I would take advantage of this opportunity?* Maybe, in an effort to take hold of an opportunity for which you're not prepared, you attempt to take the necessary steps or make the necessary changes, only to realize time has slipped away and taken the opportunity with it.

So often, we think we can do the work necessary to take advantage of an opportunity when it arises, so we fail to prepare. Let me encourage you to take action when you know it is time to act. No one can do it for you. No one can make you start a new habit. No one can make you hone your craft or sharpen your skills. You alone must set standards for yourself. You alone must take action. You know what is important to you, and these things require action every day. One More Shot people understand this truth.

Often, the most important plays in life come when you least expect them. Because of this, we've got to use *now* to our advantage. Decide right now to fix your situation and get moving. The speed with which you move will make all the difference in the world.

NOTES

It has been said, "Strike while the iron is hot." I like Oliver Cromwell's quote better: "Not only strike while the iron is hot, but make it hot by striking." In other words, be so *now* minded that your brain catches fire with opportunity and growth.

Key Questions:

What elements of your life require you to take action steps right now?

If you knew you could not fail, what actions would you take right now?

Why are you not taking action right now?

NOTES

One More Shot People Realize Time is Running Out

Benjamin Franklin had this to say about time:
"You may delay, but time will not." In other words, time
is drawing to a close for every one of us. Too many people
fail to realize this; the truth that *time is undefeated* is not
something they think about. They simply move through
their day making choices as if they will be here forever.

There was a young man who found out his wife was dying
of cancer. He asked her, "How does it feel to know you
are dying?" She looked at him and replied, "How does it
feel to think you are not?"

One More Shot people approach every situation with the
knowledge that time is running out. They have a deeper
sense of awareness of what is going on around them,
and they recognize the importance of focus. One More
Shot people focus on the things that are happening now.
They live as Kevin Elko urges us to "be where your feet
are". This approach makes it easier to not get lost in soul-
sucking things like worry, anxiety, and doubt.

I love the Billy Dean song *Only Here for a Little While*.
Read these words carefully:

Today I stood singing songs and saying, 'Amen.'

Saying goodbye to an old friend who seemed so young.

He spent his life working hard to chase a dollar.

NOTES

Putting off until tomorrow the things he should have done.

Made me stop and think what's the hurry, why the running?

I don't like what I am becoming, going to change my style.

Take my time and not take it all for granted.

Cause we are only here for a little while.

I remember the first time I put this mentality into practice in my life. We had just won our second straight softball county championship in a close game against a very good team. My typical coaching mentality was focus forward, to note things we needed to correct at the next practice and move forward in preparation for the next game.

This time, I realized how important it was to take it all in. I sat quietly on a bucket and allowed the good of the moment to sink it, as if something inside me said, "You may not have many of these left. You need to enjoy it."

If you get nothing else from this book, please get this: Time is running out. Make the most of every moment you have. Time is our most important asset. We must pay very close attention to it. It will be the one thing you will long for most as it passes by. Please be mindful of how you use it.

NOTES

This is a great formula to use:
Time divided by Intention = Fulfillment.

Key Questions:

What is your reaction to the phrase *time is running out?*

How well do you stay focused on the events, people, and days you are in?

Are you where your feet are?

NOTES

CHAPTER 2
Habits of a One More Shot Person

One More Shot People Are First to Arrive and Last to Leave

I love Elon Hilderbrand's quote: "To be early is to be on time, to be on time is late, and to be late is to be forgotten."

One More Shot people understand the importance of being early. Being fashionably late is just an excuse for average people to stay average. Being early is important because it shows respect for what is taking place. I tell my employees — and when I was coaching, I told my players — you never know what or who you will run into when you are early to an event. The extra few minutes may leave an impression that may result in positive outcomes. But it's not just arriving early to scheduled events and meetings that matters; One More Shot people understand the importance of being early to concepts as well.

Being first on the metaphorical scene of a new concept has profound implications for One More Shot people. While being the first to try something different can be intimidating, and it can bring with it new challenges, individuals who pioneer or adopt new concepts often end up stronger as a result. Showing up early to new concepts

NOTES

allows you to go through the struggles and growth necessary to achieve success and foster belief in the concept. The biggest advantage will be belief.

I know two brothers, Pat and Mike Maser, who were early to embrace a network marketing concept. Proven leaders who have made millions of dollars, Pat and Mike have been with the same company for more than 20 years and have seen thousands of representatives come and go. They are extremely profitable as a result. Why? Because they were early to a new concept, and they believed in it.

Being early caused them to struggle, grow, and believe. Read this carefully again and again: The earlier you are to a new, good concept, the more you will struggle, grow, and believe. The more you struggle, grow, and believe in a good concept, the more you experience success over time. Pat and Mike say things are so much better and easier now that the track they run on is proven.

What you will never hear them say is that you can't win by partnering with the company. You won't hear that because their belief level is so high. One More Shot people show up early to events and early to new, good concepts. This creates opportunities to go through the necessary struggles to foster belief.

NOTES

Key Questions:

What is your mindset when it comes to being early?

Do people know they can count on you to show up when you say you will be there?

What is your attitude when it comes to taking advantage of new, good concepts?

Are you willing to struggle so you can believe?

NOTES

One More Shot People Get out of their Comfort Zone to Encourage Others

I was privileged to meet a very impressive young lady named Autumn Provenzano, who was in her early 20s, friendly, and bubbling with joy. Autumn was a rising star in her company and an emerging leader. She had a quiet confidence that told me she was probably fearless. But the reality was, Autumn was afraid of public speaking. She had to put aside her fear and speak publicly in order to accomplish her goal of helping others. She did an exceptional job speaking and made a lasting impression on many people, including me.

Her actions helped me realize that encouraging others may require a person to step out of his or her comfort zone. When I think of the encouraging stories that have stuck with me over time, I realize they had one element in common; they all involve individuals who live outside of their comfort zones. A little thing like losing 10 pounds can encourage others to become healthier. Statistics show if your friend loses 10 pounds, you have a 70 percent chance of losing 10 pounds as well. Weight loss is uncomfortable and requires sacrifice, but it can be very encouraging to others.

Let this example open your mind to countless other ways you can step out of your comfort zone to encourage others. Make a list and then make a habit of living outside

NOTES

your comfort zone. No doubt, you'll encourage others and position yourself to make your shot count when given the opportunity.

Key Questions:

Who do you know who needs encouragement?

In what areas are you willing to step out of your comfort zone to encourage others?

NOTES

One More Shot People Are Serious About Physical Fitness

This one is challenging, but it can be the most rewarding. When I began to take my own fitness journey seriously, it was easy to stay motivated because I set obtainable goals. However, I achieved only some of those goals because I focused solely on the outcomes I desired and not the habits that would have led to sustainable success. I didn't focus on adapting my habits to becoming a person for whom fitness is a lifestyle. So, once I reached my goals, within a few months I reverted to unfocused behaviors. I worked out regularly, but my diet was inconsistent.

I realized I had to shift my focus, so I moved away from the "goal of accomplishing goals" and refocused on changing my lifestyle. As a result, my fitness routine became an area of my life that is non-negotiable. I would encourage you to invest some time and money into becoming physically fit and make it part of your lifestyle.

Now for the cold hard truth. This will not be easy if you are new to the world of physical fitness or have been slacking for a while. If I could offer advice from my own experience, I suggest you find a plan that suits you and fits your lifestyle. Find something you can do every day that challenges you. Yes, that says *every day*. I would completely forget about goals and be mindful of *today* every day.

NOTES

By focusing less on your goals and more on the creation of a lifestyle, you'll eventually reach your goals by default. In doing so, you will position yourself to be ready mentally and physically when the shot you need to take presents itself.

Truthfully, most of us know what we need to do, but we lack discipline to do it. Those genuinely new to the practices of physical fitness will find a million helpful instruction videos on YouTube. Pick one. Get started.

You know what to eat. Start eating right today. Trust me, when it comes time to take your shot, you will be glad you have this element under control.

A few things you should anticipate:

When you start, you will be sore the first few weeks while your body adjusts.

You will crave all the stuff you know you should not eat.

There is the possibility for injury. When this happens, adjust, and adapt and keep moving.

Do something every day to get fit. Again, you already know what to do. It's very important to start doing it.

NOTES

Key questions:

What is your current physical fitness level?

What are you currently doing to improve your fitness?

Do you have fitness goals, or are you a fit person living a lifestyle of fitness?

Will you start today?

NOTES

One More Shot People Read Every Day

The habit of reading every day – specifically reading non-fiction – is not only important for taking and making your shot count, it is vital. Read things that encourage, instruct, and teach. Reading can truly open new worlds. You can explore and learn about things that most people will never personally see or experience.

By now, you're probably thinking *what is up with this every day stuff? Why do we need to read every day?* I assume you are reading this book for a reason. You are in a situation where you need to take a shot, and you must make the shot count. If that is you, reading daily will greatly improve your chances of success.

So, what do you need to read? I encourage you to start with the book of Proverbs in the *Bible.* You will gain wisdom and insight into how each of us should respond to the world around us. My favorite chapter is chapter 12. There are 31 short chapters in the book, making it easy for you to read all of Proverbs in a month if you read one chapter every day. I do this on a recurring basis.

When you finish Proverbs, I encourage you to read the Gospel of John; it will open your eyes to who Jesus is. After that, other books I would read in this order are as follows: *How to Win Friends and Influence People,* by Dale Carnegie; *Flip the Switch,* by Michael Burt; *Atomic Habits,* by James Clear; *The Ideal Team Player,* by

NOTES

Patrick Lencioni; and *The Power of One More,* by Ed Mylett. These books will give you a solid foundation for your journey to become a mentally strong One More Shot person.

After completing that list, consider reading books by John Maxwell, Andy Andrews, and Simon Sinek. These three authors will help you continue the journey and, simply by reviewing the footnotes found in their books, broaden your own library.

Reading daily can benefit you profoundly in ways you might not expect.

Some friends and I were putting up tree stands on a farm we lease to hunt deer. As I was attaching a ratchet strap to the stand, I had a hard time getting it straight and tight. My friends tried teaching me the proper way to do it, but I was not doing a very good job taking instruction. I became frustrated, and the next day I refused to do the ratchet straps.

The following day was the 12th of the month, which means I was reading Proverbs chapter 12. Proverbs 12:1 (NKJV) says, "Whoever loves instruction loves knowledge, but he who hates correction is stupid." The day before, I did not enjoy the correction of my friends, even though it was for my benefit. However, because I had developed the habit of reading every day, I learned a very valuable lesson from that experience.

NOTES

By reading daily, you grow in ways you can't even imagine. You never know when something you read will impact your life. The more you read, the more ways you will find to apply what you've learned in your own life.

Key Questions:

What are you currently reading?

How often do you read?

How long has it been since something you have read has had an impact on your life?

NOTES

One More Shot People Have a Very Grateful Heart

I met Mrs. Bates, the mother of my business partner, when she was 80 years old. She had recently lost her husband of 60 years. They raised three children, and all three kids grew up to be great adults who are raising wonderful children of their own. In my first encounter with Mrs. Bates, I could tell she was different. She used her words intentionally to encourage me, and she showed a genuine interest in what I was doing. She asked about my family. She told me she was praying for us and that I was making a real impact at the office. She was very deliberate with her praise. She told me how much she appreciated me. Every encounter with her over the next year was the same, very intentional and very encouraging.

When Mrs. Bates passed away at the age of 82, I was not shocked to see the size of the crowd at her funeral, and I was not surprised by the words of the individuals who spoke about how much she encouraged them. She was a world-class encourager. I offered my condolences to my business partner on the loss of his mother, but my sadness went beyond concern for my friend. I was sad for the world because Mrs. Bates was one of the special ones who honed her gift into a special skill she used to encouraged everyone she encountered.

At our Christmas party the year she passed, Bruce read the last words his mother wrote in her journal, a prayer she closed with these words: "From a person with a very

NOTES

grateful heart." As he shared those words, I noted they bore witness to the foundation which enabled her to be a pillar of encouragement for so many. That foundation was a very grateful heart.

Baptist Health did a study and reported the findings in a 2021 article titled "The Power of a Grateful Heart." The study revealed:

Gratitude can improve general well-being, increase resilience, strengthen relationships, reduce stress, and mitigate depression. Gratitude multiplies the neurochemicals that help the brain shift from thinking negatively to thinking positively. The release of dopamine, oxytocin, and serotonin leads to feelings of closeness, connection, and happiness. According to the study:

1. Gratitude helps create and improve relationships.

2. Gratitude improves physical and psychological health.

3. Gratitude enhances empathy and reduces aggression.

4. Grateful people sleep better.

5. Gratitude improves self-esteem.

6. Gratitude increases mental strength.

I don't know about you, but those are all the things I want in my life. So how do we develop a very grateful heart?

NOTES

The first thing we can do might seem small, but it is possibly the most important and easiest thing on the list to accomplish: begin each morning thanking God for another day.

I once asked a very successful coach what it was about his morning routine that allowed him to have so much energy and enthusiasm throughout the day, and his response was, "When I wake up each morning, I thank God for allowing me to have another day." Realizing today is a gift and being thankful for it is at the core of a grateful heart.

The second thing is to make a list of the things for which you are thankful. Make sure you put it in writing and keep it somewhere you can see it throughout the day. By keeping this list close and visible, you will be able to add to it as you develop a heart that is more and more grateful. It is important to look daily for things to add to this gratitude list. This fosters an attitude of gratitude.

The third thing — if you have people in your life you are close to, and I hope you do — take time to write them a handwritten note. It doesn't need to be a long note, just something letting them know you are grateful for them.

A leading growth expert for realtors says, "If you want to be on the top of the averages in real-estate sales, write two thank you notes a day." I will go one step further. If you want to be a person with a very grateful heart, write two thank you notes per day. Not only will they mean a

NOTES

lot to the recipients, but the practice will serve as a daily reminder of how much these individuals mean to you.

The fourth thing is to journal. In my own experience, this is the step that requires the most discipline to become habitual, but it will prove to be a source of gratitude and freedom.

During my tenure as a principal, I wrote down the difficult situations and conflicts I encountered. I started it for documentation, but one day when I was dealing with a very difficult situation, I read back through the previous entries and realized I had come through some difficult times. I was doing ok. A sense of calm and genuine gratitude came over me as I realized what I was going through would only make me stronger. I now keep a journal for the good and bad. It helps to look back on where I've been and promotes thankfulness within me as a result.

Key Questions:

What are you thankful for?

Are you starting each day thanking God for a new day?

Do you have a list of things and people you are thankful for?

NOTES

CHAPTER 3
Attitude Development of a One More Shot Person

It had been a long day. As I pulled into the driveway, I noticed a dead armadillo on the ground beside the mailbox. I did what any self-respecting man would do after a long day at work … I ignored it.

But I was not the one who checked the mail. Cindy did. And she had seen the armadillo and insisted it should be taken care of quickly. So, I went right back out the door, shovel in hand, to get rid of the armadillo. I thought to myself, *I need to dig a hole and bury this thing.* Then I thought, *I can just scoop it up and take it to the end of the long, deep ditch and throw it in there.*

Problem solved.

About a week later, I took the trash can down to the end of the driveway. The trash truck came and went, and before I got home from work that evening, we received more than two inches of rain. When I finally made it home, I noticed the trash can had fallen into the ditch. I worked my way down the bank to retrieve it, and when I pulled it up, the lid flipped over and soaked me with dead armadillo water. The smell was horrible. It was on

NOTES

me, it was in my truck, and when I went into the house, Cindy pointed out that I smelled horrible. It was so bad I had to take my clothes off and wash them outside.

Here is what I realized: A bad attitude is like dead armadillo water. If you do not properly take care of it, it will eventually get all over you. Your environment will stink, and everyone around you will notice.

So how do we properly handle a bad attitude?

Identify the Bad Attitude

I want to begin with a truth that will make most people uncomfortable. There are two ways bad attitudes are identified. The first one is easy and should be the quickest. Most of the time we identify it ourselves; we know we have a bad attitude. We are critical, moody, our body language is terrible, and everyone is wrong about everything.

The second is when other people point out that we have a bad attitude. While we may be okay with the first one, the second one often makes our bad attitude worse — just like the dead armadillo beside the mailbox. I noticed it and thought it would be okay to let it lie, so I wasn't happy when Cindy asked me to do something about it.

To identify a bad attitude, it helps to understand the difference between a good one and a bad one. A person with a good attitude will approach challenges,

NOTES

circumstances, and interactions with optimism and constructive thinking, while someone with a bad attitude will fail to acknowledge the good and focus on the bad in people, situations, events, etc.

Most of us would say our attitude is pretty good most of the time. But what happens when you read those definitions? Do you reconsider? Do people, situations, and events ever create issues for you? If so, how do you respond? Do you approach those situations with optimism, or do you focus on the bad? The first step in developing a great attitude is to identify your own attitude now.

Key Questions:

Are you intentional about identifying your attitude daily?

Do you have optimism in difficult interactions?

Are you a constructive thinker or do you just accept your current situation?

NOTES

Dig a Hole

Dig a hole. This is how you make that unwanted attitude go away properly.

Not literally, you don't need to go outside and dig a hole. But mentally — figuratively — you need to dig a hole. Visualize yourself digging. That is the mental picture you need if you're going to take care of the bad attitude. Had I taken the time to dig a hole when I encountered the armadillo, odds are, I would have disposed of it properly and permanently the first time.

When you're digging this mental hole, there are several things you'll want to keep in mind. First, make sure you identify anything you could hit while digging that would cause your bad attitude to escalate. In our state, we call 811 before we dig. This service makes sure we don't hit the wrong thing when we dig, ensuring what needs to stay buried stays buried. When you dig, the situation will worsen if you dig without thinking first. If you start your mental digging and old, unwanted memories or problems start coming to mind, visualize moving over and digging in a new location. Remember, you are only trying to bury a bad attitude; you're not trying to resolve problems from the past.

NOTES

The second thing you need to do is to make sure you dig the hole deep enough. The worst attitudes need the deepest holes, and you don't want that attitude clawing its way to the surface. Dig deep.

Third, make sure the hole is big enough for the situation you are dealing with. You are the only one who knows the size of your bad attitude. What you are dealing with may seem small to others, but in your mind, it's much bigger. You're the only one who can decide how big that hole should be.

Key Questions:

What bad attitudes are you holding onto in your mind?

Are you willing to deal with these bad attitudes properly?

It all starts by visualizing and digging a mental hole. Will you dig the hole?

NOTES

Bury the BAD Attitude

This one will seem counter to the culture we live in. Contemporary culture tells us to "let it all out." The present mindset of many today would suggest that whatever you do, make sure you don't bury it, because it will eventually arise. That is great advice for a lot of things we deal with, but not a bad attitude.

Remember, bad attitudes stink. They get all over you and make your environment stink, and they make others aware of the fact that you stink. The right thing to do is bury the bad attitude. Start by visualizing yourself scooping the bad attitude up and putting it in the hole. Make sure it hits bottom. Then – here's the fun part — use the shovel to fill the hole. Make sure the dirt is packed down.

The next step is important. Tuck the shovel away someplace way back in the corner of your mind where you can find it when you need to bury another bad attitude. Under no circumstances should you use it to dig up the one you just buried. Let it rest in peace.

But what about situations where a recurring bad attitude seems to plague you? How do you handle situations where the same bad attitude comes back up again and again? The answer is rather simple. Mentally go back to the spot where you buried it and say to yourself:

NOTES

That attitude is out of my life.

I buried it right here.

It's dead; it's rotten; it stinks.

I refuse to dig it up.

If you find yourself tempted to dig, visualize having to crawl back into the darkest recesses of your mind where you stowed away the shovel, and tell yourself: *It's not worth the trouble. I'm not digging that back up.*

Now move forward and forget about it.

My wife Cindy is a CPA and gifted when it comes to business finance. I am not gifted in that area. She tries to suggest sound financial practices for my businesses, and sometimes I struggle with my attitude during those conversations. I need to bury that bad attitude and have an adult conversation with my very qualified wife.
My problem is, I have not buried that attitude. Every time the conversation comes up, my bad attitude interferes with what should be a profitable conversation. If I just bury the attitude and listen, our business meetings will be much more productive.

NOTES

Key Questions:

What are some bad attitudes you need to bury?

Are you willing to put them in the hole?

Will you commit to not digging them back up?

NOTES

Set Your Triggers

A "trigger" is simply a stimulus that elicits a reaction or response. It can initiate symptoms of a problem or worsen them.

Stop and think about your attitude. What are some things that cause your attitude to improve? What are the external factors that cause you to have a great attitude? The answers will be different for everyone. I encourage you to list those things and then mentally put big red buttons all over your body that say, "push me." Look for ways to engage people in conversations that will activate your triggers.

On the other hand, you must also be aware of things that trigger a bad attitude. I recommend being deliberate in how you treat those triggers. On the way to work, school, home, church, etc. — wherever you encounter people who can trigger bad attitudes — take time to set those triggers in hard-to-reach places.

While the visual for good attitudes should be bright red push-me buttons that are easily accessible, the things that trigger bad attitudes should be visualized with buttons that are difficult to see and reach. Make them much smaller than the big red buttons that trigger a good attitude. By doing this consistently over time, you will begin to have fewer and fewer bad attitudes to bury.

NOTES

That said, no matter how hard you work to hide them and no matter how hard you work to find and set the correct responses, there will be people who are naturally gifted at finding the bad attitude buttons. These people will walk right up, push your button, and trigger a bad attitude like it's their job. When this happens, identify it, dig a hole, and bury it quickly. Reset your triggers. Hide your button and move forward.

For illustrative purposes, imagine you're on your way to the office, where you know you will have a difficult meeting that could go in a way that causes the other person to make personal, critical, or challenging remarks to you. They could intentionally try to move your attitude from good to bad. The easy thing to do would be to come up with the negative response, but I encourage you to set your triggers ahead of time.

If the other person puts you in a bad attitude response situation, you can choose ahead of time how you will respond by setting your triggers to cue a different response. Maybe you can respond to their negative comments with a follow-up question, or perhaps you will ignore them altogether, simply choosing to take the high road, remaining calm and professional. A word of caution to that end: Most of the time, people will continue to push if you take the high road. It will take them a couple of minutes of pushing before they realize you are going to stay up there on the high road, and they will — for the most part — calm down.

NOTES

Key Questions:

Do you have people or events that trigger bad attitudes in your life?

Are you willing to take time to identify your triggers ahead of time?

Will you take time to set and reset your triggers ahead of time?

NOTES

Adjust

When it comes to maintaining a good attitude, there is one final piece of the puzzle. You must *adjust*. There are three key areas in life that frequently need an adjustment: mindset, focus, and belief. It's important to understand how adjustments to each of these areas are necessary if we are to maintain a consistently good attitude.

The mindset adjustment can be described best with the analogy of — you guessed it — a hole! Picture this: You're walking down the street and fall into a hole. People see this happen and come to help you out of it. Your response to them goes something like, "I didn't see the hole." A few weeks later, you walk down the same street and fall into the same hole. Like last time, people come to your aid. Your response this time is, "I thought they would have fixed that hole by now." You move on with your life.

A few weeks later, you walk down that street for the third time, and though you clearly see the hole, you fall in it again. Why? Perhaps because you know people will help you and by now, you are comfortable in the hole.

Eventually, you get tired of falling into the same hole, so when you walk down that street, you walk around it. You think to yourself, "I am doing such a good job avoiding the hole." But seeing that hole triggers unpleasant memories and emotions you want to avoid,

NOTES

so you decide to take a different street entirely.
The mindset shift is taking a different street.

Put more practically, maybe your boss is always
challenging you and you assume he or she hates you.
A simple mindset shift allows you to assume your boss
sees your potential and desires to push you to become the
best you can be at your job. This mindset shift causes you
to come to work prepared.

Or perhaps you play a sport, and the coach plays another
player in your position this week. You think to yourself,
"I guess I'm not good enough" or "I'll just sit over here on
the bench and be jealous of the person playing in front
of me." But a mindset shift allows you to think, "This is
a great opportunity for me to encourage my teammates.
This gives me the chance to focus on my skills in practice
to compete for my position. By doing this, I will become a
better teammate and player." The mindset shift is a small
adjustment that makes a big difference.

The second adjustment necessary to promote a
consistently good attitude is an adjustment of focus.
What you focus on determines what you get. Let me
explain. If you focus on the negative in a situation, odds
are, even if you do not ultimately experience a negative
outcome, you will have spent your time internalizing the
possibility of a negative, which will directly impact how
you experience the situation. This one is difficult because
negativity is the easiest place for the mind to go.

NOTES

Say, for example, if the doctor tells you that you have
cancer, your initial reaction may be to focus on the
negative and become anxious and scared, which will cause
a mental and physical response that leaves you feeling
down and discouraged. On the other hand, if you focus
on taking your cancer diagnosis one step at a time and
look for the best possible outcome at each step, you will
have hope and purpose. This will leave you in a position
to encourage others even through your own difficulty.

Oprah Winfrey has this to say about focus: "What you
focus on expands — when you focus on the goodness in
your life, you create more of it."

Adjust and focus on the good even in difficult situations.

The final adjustment is belief. Do you believe it before you
see it, or must you see it to believe it? I encourage you to
adjust your default to believing it before you see it. In doing
so, you will give yourself a leg up when it comes to attitude.

This will also keep you from living in someone else's
house. Let me explain. If you buy a house that has already
been constructed, you are living in what someone else
envisioned. You are living in what that person was able to
see and build. This analogy applies to your belief in your
life. When you adjust to believing first and then seeing,
you will develop the life you are looking for not the life

NOTES

someone else constructs for you. Walt Disney said, "If you can visualize it, if you can dream it — there is some way to do it." Can you see it?

When you make these adjustments, the things you deal with that once triggered bad attitudes will submit to your new mindset, focus, and belief. This will allow you to see the good in every situation and promote a positive attitude as the default attitude in your life.

Key Questions:

What is the mindset shift you need to make for your daily life to improve?

In what areas do you need to change your focus?

What are the positive things in your life you can focus on?

Have you given up on believing things can happen positively for you?

Are you looking for people and events that will help you keep believing?

What are the things you believe about your future right now?

NOTES

A bad attitude is like dead armadillo water. A good attitude is a spring of life that encourages others and creates freedom.

Proverbs 17:22 says "A joyful Heart is good medicine, but a crushed spirit dries up the bones" (ESV).

My friend Michael Crowder is a very successful businessman. He has started 12 companies, and seven of those companies have earned more than seven figures annually. What separates Michael from other business owners is his incredible attitude. He is always positive, always encouraging. Even when he is coaching, Michael reaches in and pulls out the best of himself, and his positive attitude shines through.

Most impressively, Michael's amazing wife and kids exhibit the same attitude. They all make people feel welcome and important in every encounter. It's not an act; the Crowder family genuinely cares for people, and the attitudes they exhibit daily are their calling cards. This is a testimony to their father and his commitment to having the best possible attitude he can bring to the world each day. He is a picture of what a successful businessman and father should be.

Your takeaway from this chapter should be that no matter what you are trying to accomplish, if your attitude is correct, you have a great opportunity to be successful, and those around you will grow as a result. Remember, a bad attitude is like dead armadillo water.

NOTES

CHAPTER 4
You Missed Your Shot

Michael Jordan missed 26 game-winning shots. Kobe Bryant missed 14,481 shots in his NBA career. The overall batting average for players in the MLB Hall of Fame is .303. In sports, the best in the world miss opportunities every day.

It is the same in life. You can probably list some shots you've missed. I believe those fall into one of three categories.

1. You missed the shot because of your own mistakes or lack of preparation. You were not ready for the shot you were given. On one hand, this is my least favorite because this one is controllable. On the other hand, it's also my favorite missed shot scenario because you can control it in the future.

2. You missed your shot because of other people. You were prepared to take the shot but someone else caused you to lose the opportunity to be successful for a multitude of reasons.

NOTES

3. You missed your shot because the world is a messed-up place. Sometimes you are ready for the opportunity, people are encouraging, helpful, and supportive, but the world interferes. This one is completely out of our control and simply a part of life.

So, what do you do when you have missed your shot?

Get a Good Coach

I have three coaches. One is coaching me in physical fitness, one is helping me scale my service business, and my third coach is helping me become a more effective coach myself. These three men challenge me daily to become more than I am capable of on my own. I am significantly more successful in the areas I am being coached than I am in other areas of my life.

One of my coaches, Michael Burt, says "Everyone needs a good coach in their lives. A good coach does three things for you. They will have conversations with you that you may or may not want to have. They are going to help you do some things you may or may not want to do. They are going to help you become something you did not think you could become."

I believe with all that I am that those words are more than true. In fact, if you take them to heart and find a good coach for your life, you'll find that this concept is life changing.

NOTES

I watched a video about Christian McCaffrey's preseason workout. He had a strength coach and a physiology coach. Each coach had a specific area of focus, and Christian was listening to every word each one said to him. Why would a top NFL running back have two coaches at his workout? He understands his best opportunity for success is to have coaches who challenge him to do more and be more in specific areas.

If a top athlete understands the importance of having multiple coaches in his life, how much more should you be seeking a good coach in your life? We are only given one life. To be the best possible version of yourself, to have the best opportunity to make your next shot, you need a good coach. Listening to podcasts and reading books like this one will only take you so far. To become a professional, to stop treating your life like a hobby, you will need someone to pull the best out of you.

I like to play golf. I'm self-taught. I never took a lesson, never had a coach, and I had no instructions. When I played regularly, I would go to the range, hit some balls or maybe play a round. Golf always costs me money.

Scottie Scheffler, on the other hand, is currently the number one golfer in the world. Through his first 10 events in 2023, he made 11 million dollars just from golf earnings, not including endorsements. Scottie has a swing coach, a nutrition coach, a strength and conditioning coach, a mindset coach, and a financial coach.

NOTES

There is clearly a difference in how we approach the game. Golf is his profession, and golf is my hobby. Again, your life is too important to treat it like a hobby. Get a coach. Go pro.

Key Questions:

What shot are you getting ready to take in life?

Do you have a good coach helping you prepare to take that shot?

In what areas of your life do you feel that having a coach would benefit you the most?

NOTES

Emotions/Feelings

So, you missed your shot. Now come the emotions. You are already reading the book, so I don't need to promote it to you, but I can tell you that the first three chapters will help you through the various emotions you'll experience throughout your life when it comes to missing a shot. That being said, they won't stop those emotions from coming at you, but that's not the goal. The goal is for you to be better prepared to handle them when they do show up.

There are several things you need to know about the emotions you experience when you miss a shot. First, be aware that your emotions may range from "Oh, I can't believe I missed that opportunity" to "I can't breathe!" When you miss a big shot in life, anger, fear, remorse, panic, and sadness can flood in like a raging river.

The smaller less significant shots trigger a lesser range of emotions. Most of the time, these will take care of themselves in a couple of days, and you can move on. However, I want to caution you about moving on without learning from the experience. It is very important to learn the lessons that seemingly insignificant missed shots can teach you. Studying these lessons will help you avoid missing bigger shots in the future.

Missing a big shot is an entirely different experience. These emotions can take months and even years to overcome. These emotions can cause two major problems.

NOTES

First, they can cause you to lose time when you get so caught up in your emotions that you fail to realize time is still moving. The clock is still ticking. If you are not careful, you can lose precious time while caught up in your emotions.

The second thing is, you may fail to realize that you cannot take an effective shot when you are caught up in your feelings.

Those things will cause you to make decisions outside of your normal response. Say, for example, you miss your big shot, and you are angry, hurt, and depressed. God clears a path and creates your next big shot, a life-changing opportunity. You walk away. You just don't feel like doing "it" right now. You are afraid you will get hurt again, so you move away from the opportunity. When you read that, you might assume I'm advocating for the "get back in the game" approach. I am not saying you need to simply take the next available shot; I'm saying take the next shot that God provides.

So how do you effectively deal with emotions, so you don't waste time and miss shots? First, make sure you live in the day you're in. Kevin Elko says, "Be where your feet are." It's okay to look back; it's not okay to *live* back. You can't relive yesterday physically, so stop doing it mentally.

Second, do something challenging — something outside your comfort zone that will help you become a better

NOTES

person. Doing hard things gives us the courage to move forward. This will help you begin to move from feelings to actions. The more you act, even when you don't feel like it, the less your feelings control you.

Finally, take every opportunity to grow personally. This is the one area that will allow you to move beyond emotions. You may not be able to change them, but you can outgrow them. The emotions and feelings will show up. Prepare ahead of time.

Key questions:

Are you having trouble dealing with emotions and feelings from a big, missed shot?

How much time have you lost dealing with your emotions?

Can you make your next shot with the emotions you are currently dealing with?

If not, what do you need to change now?

NOTES

Evaluate

I love this quote by Aaron Ramsdale: "When we win, we celebrate, and if we don't, then we evaluate it and go again." Evaluation is needed in every area of our life. Evaluation is internal. Sure, we can look on the outside and see what is visible. We can even compare that outward appearance to others. Nowadays, we can even use filters and social media to make the outside look better, but the inside is a different story.

Our pastor says often, "I shave me every day." In other words, I see what I am in the mirror every day. The good news is, we are seldom as good or as bad as we think we are. So, when it comes to your missed shot, what do you need to evaluate?

First, look at your fundamentals. These are your basic core values. I have three.

1. Go the extra mile. I want to show up and deliver more than is expected.
2. Add value to people. Find a way to help others feel wanted, needed, accepted, and encouraged.
3. Be a Christ-like example by showing up and representing my savior in an honorable and worthy way.

NOTES

I have missed some really big shots in my life, and when I go back and evaluate, I use these three filters. Every miss can be traced back to falling short on one or more of these core values.

What are your fundaments? If you do not have them listed, stop reading and write them down. You cannot properly evaluate if you do not understand your fundamentals.

Next, look at your habits. Are your habits producing the product you want to present to the world? You will also need to check your attitude. Have you allowed the unwanted, terrible attitude to start to stink? Finally, look at how you handle time. Time is a precious gift; make sure you treat it as such.

It is very important to review each of these every time you miss an important shot. It would be a shame to get into the first one and discover the absence of a key fundamental is causing you to stop there and miss your next shot because you were also missing some key habits. For this to be effective, you need to perform a full evaluation. Without proper evaluation, the odds of improvement and making your next shot count are very low.

NOTES

Key Questions:

Do you have your fundamentals listed on paper?

Are you effectively evaluating your missed shots?

If so, what does that process look like for you?

Are you using evaluation when preparing for your next shot?

NOTES

Plan

Now for the good stuff. You have your coach in place; you're working on those emotions; and you have carefully evaluated your missed shot. Now it's time to plan for your next shot.

Every effective plan has three steps:

1. Make a plan.
2. Follow the plan.
3. Implement the plan.

I am sure most of you have tried to put something together that came in pieces in a box. Obviously, the correct approach is to open the box, locate and read the instructions, and follow them. You know that opening a box and finding no instructions can lead to disaster. The bigger and more complex the project, the greater the potential for disaster. If you have the instructions and do not use them, it can lead to disaster. What happens if you have the instructions and read them but then don't follow them? The correct answer is nothing. The item remains in pieces. When you start to plan, you must keep these things in mind.

For a plan to be effective, it's critical to start with the end in mind. If you are interested in making your next shot, you need to make sure you know what it looks like to make that shot. I encourage you to visualize what

NOTES

it will look like and feel like when you make the shot. Doing this before you plan will energize you through the planning process.

Look for the details that give you the best opportunity to make your shot. Pay close attention to the things you often overlook, ignore, or consider insignificant. Get your coach involved in the process from the beginning. When you have someone who can guide, push, and encourage you through the planning process, your odds of making the shot increase exponentially. There's no magic to this. Write your plan on paper, put it in a place where you can see it, and follow the plan.

It's important to set realistic goals. I struggle in this area. I'll start the process — my plan is ready, and I begin to implement it, but I don't give serious consideration to how long it will take to accomplish my goal. Often, it's harder than I anticipate, and therefore, it takes more time. This leads me to think the plan isn't going to work. Be careful to avoid this. In your plan, include daily actions that will keep you on track to take advantage of your next shot opportunity.

Key Questions:

What are you currently planning for?

Is your coach helping you plan?

Can you visualize what it looks like to fully implement your plan?

NOTES

Reload

I love this part because I love this story. I am a deer
hunter — not a deer killer, just a hunter. This means I
watch way more deer than I shoot. I enjoy being outdoors
and taking in all the goodness that nature has to offer.

Once, during a hunting trip to Kentucky, my friends and
I went out on a very cold, windy morning. We planned to
stay until 9:30 that morning, but I was shivering sitting in
the stand. So, I did the best thing I could do to get warmer;
I climbed down. When I made it to the ground, I saw
a deer walking toward me. I took careful aim with my
muzzleloader and pulled the trigger. All I heard was *click.*

I had forgotten to put the primer in. As quickly as possible,
I pulled a primer out of my bag, put it in, and pulled the
trigger again. This time, my firing pin struck the primer
and there was a delay before the gun went off. When the
smoke cleared, the deer was still walking down the trail.
I took my time, reloaded, and aimed again. The same
thing happened. The primer went off, then came a long
delay, and then the gun fired, and I missed again.

The hungry deer didn't seem concerned that I stood
between her and the corn. I believe she felt completely
safe, even with me shooting at her. I reloaded, fired, and
got the same results. The deer walked around me and
started eating corn.

NOTES

I would like to tell you I finally took a good shot and killed the deer, but it didn't happen that way. The deer kept eating corn, and I walked back to the truck empty-handed and out of bullets.

I tell that story for a couple of reasons. First, it illustrates the point that you need to take time to reload properly. When you rush the reload, you stand a good chance of misfiring. Also, you need to make sure you always have enough bullets. It does not feel good to have a target in sight and realize you are out of bullets.

In life, how can you reload and how can you make sure that you always have enough bullets? I believe the best way to prepare for any reload situation is to have a time daily when you read God's word and pray to him. These two things done consistently will equip you with the right ammunition to reload when you miss a shot.

As I wrote earlier, the best place to start is by reading a chapter in Proverbs each day and a chapter in the book of John. These two books will provide the foundation for everything else you will learn in the future by reading God's word. If you've been on earth for any length of time, chances are good that you've missed a shot or two. Some shots are big, some are small, but they all matter. Reload through the wonderful power of God's word.

NOTES

Key Questions:

Are you studying God's word? If so, are you intentional?

Have you come to a situation where you are out of bullets?
If so, have you started studying God's word?

If you can't reload, you can't take your next shot.
What are you doing to make reloading more efficient?

NOTES

CONCLUSION

For football fans in the United States, there is a moment etched in history. Super Bowl XXV on January 7, 1991, at Tampa Stadium. The Buffalo Bills versus the New York Giants. The game was back and forth, and both teams gave their very best, but it all came down to one kick. The ball was placed on the 40-yard line to set up a 47-yard field goal attempt by the Bills' Scott Norwood.

Buffalo was down by a single point, 20 to 19, with a few seconds remaining in the game. The snap and hold were perfect. The swing of Norwood's leg was pure – his foot made a solid, clean connection with the ball. The kick was up and sailed wide right. He missed the goal post by mere inches, and the Giants won the Super Bowl. In an instant, Scott Norwood became linked to one of the biggest missed opportunities in sports history.

ESPN did a 30 for 30 on the Bills, and a big part of that story focused on the kick – the famous missed opportunity. I would have expected the negative publicity to have been unbearable for Norwood. No doubt, it was a terrible experience, but have a look at his response. He said in regard to the kick, "I've got to tell you right now that we're all struggling with this right now. We all realize the sun's going to come up tomorrow, and we're going to start preparing this football team."

NOTES

He went on to say:

"The greatest glory in living lies is not in never falling, but in rising every time we fall."

"Failure is not fatal, but failure to change might be."

"Champions are not made in the spotlight but in the darkness of perseverance and dedication."

"You miss one hundred percent of the shots you don't take."

"I've learned that adversity is not a roadblock, but instead a stepping stone to greatness."

Having missed the biggest kick of his career, one that cost the Buffalo Bills the Super Bowl, Norwood's attitude was remarkable. Where did it come from?

It came from knowing he was prepared. It came from the knowledge that he had given his all to prepare for that moment. Did it still hurt? Absolutely. Did it still affect his teammates? No doubt. Did it leave him completely broken? Not at all. Why? Because in it, he had no regrets.

My mission from the start of this book has been to help you live your life with no regrets going forward. There is no guarantee that even if perfectly prepared you will make

NOTES

your next shot count. But even if you miss a shot — as long as you are prepared for it — you can live like Scott Norwood on the *at least* side of things.

At least I gave my best effort.

At least I made the most of my time.

At least my habits are working for me.

At least my attitude is great.

At least I saw it through to the end.

At least I can take pride in the experience and growth.

This mentality, even in the midst of perceived failure, leads to confidence, the confidence necessary to take One More Shot, and that's what counts.

NOTES

NOTES